What is the Lord's Supper?

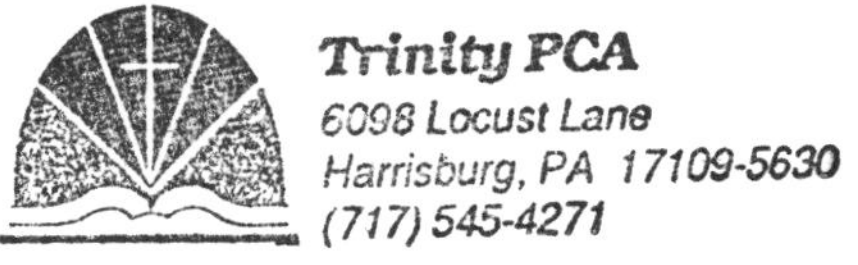

Basics of the Reformed Faith

Also available in the series:

What Is a True Calvinist?
What Is a Reformed Church?
What Is True Conversion?

What Is the Lord's Supper?

Richard D. Phillips

P&R
PUBLISHING
P.O. BOX 817 • PHILLIPSBURG • NEW JERSEY 08865-0817

Italics within Scripture quotations indicate emphasis added.

Page design by Tobias Design
Typesetting by Dawn Premako

Printed in the United States of America

Library of Congress Cataloging-in-Publication Data

Phillips, Richard D. (Richard Davis), 1960–
What is the Lord's supper? / Richard D. Phillips
p. c.m.—(Basics of the Reformed faith)
Includes bibliographical references.
ISBN 0-87552-647-0 (pbk.)
1. Lord's Supper—Reformed Church. 2. Reformed Church—Doctrines. I. Title. II. Series.

BX9423.C5P45 2005
234'163—dc22

2004057511

Imagine if our Lord Jesus, on the night before his arrest and crucifixion, had gathered his closest disciples and shown them a worship practice by which they were to remember him after he was gone. This ordinance would also serve to promote a spiritual bond among the believers and enshrine the meaning of the death Jesus was about to endure. We can only imagine how significant these instructions would be to the disciples in the years to come and how important a role this worship practice would play in the life of the church.

Those familiar with the Gospel accounts will realize that this is not a hypothetical situation. Jesus did, in fact, establish a sacred worship practice—a sacrament—that would center the Christian faith upon his atoning death and unite the believers in their communion with him during all the long years between his death and his second coming. As we would imagine, this sacrament, the Lord's Supper, has indeed occupied a central role in the faith and practice of the church.

All this is to highlight the oddity that so many believers, especially in contemporary evangelical Christianity, think so little of the Lord's Supper. They seldom observe it and assign to it little significance. They are largely ignorant of the theology poured into and out from it. They derive no assurance or comfort, and seek no grace, as they receive from the Lord's

Table. How remarkable this is among those supposedly devoted to the Bible!

There are, I think, two explanations for this, and both are poor excuses. First, to many evangelicals, lingering in the sacramental air is the specter of Roman Catholicism, with its mystical and ritualistic devotion to the Mass. Evangelicals therefore make the mistake of defining themselves in opposition to Rome instead of in conformity to the Bible. Thus, while unable to reject the Lord's Supper without obviously opposing the Bible, many evangelicals think that the longer the lids are kept on the better.

The second reason is the evangelicals' devotion to the Bible as the principal means of grace. Yes, Jesus established the sacrament on the night of his arrest. But after his resurrection and ascension he sent the apostles into the world as preachers of the gospel. The Book of Acts does not present the apostles as men standing before the world with trays of crackers and goblets of grape juice. Rather, they stood with the Old Testament in their hands and with the message of Christ burning in their hearts and bursting from their lips and pens. Our proper emphasis on believing Bible truth—and our less proper focus on evangelism over Christian growth—produces a coolness to the Bible's idea of sacramental grace.

The challenge before today's evangelicals, and especially those who embrace Reformed Theology, is that we should give the Lord's Supper the place intended for it by our Lord. This will mean affirming a primacy in our ministry of the Word of God, as demonstrated in the example of the apostles. But it also means restoring to our worship and our approach to spiritual growth a grateful and believing partaking of the Supper of our Lord. The goal of this booklet is to provide the understanding we need by considering the biblical institution of this sacrament, followed by a compact treatment of theological issues, and concluding with pastoral considerations for administering and receiving this blessed means of grace.

THE BIBLICAL INSTITUTION

The Lord's Supper receives its name from Paul's usage in 1 Corinthians 11:20. Other common names deriving from Scripture are the *Eucharist* (from 1 Cor. 11:24) and *Holy Communion* (from 1 Cor. 10:16). The Roman Catholic term *Mass* comes from the Latin word *missa*, used for dismissing people at the end of the Latin liturgy. There is no biblical support for this term.

The Reformers emphasized that a sacrament—that is, a sacred mystery prescribed for our worship—must have been instituted immediately by our Lord. In three parallel accounts of the Last Supper, we find Jesus' institution of this sacrament (Matt. 26:26–30; Mark 14:22–26; Luke 22:19–20), to which Paul adds a fourth account (1 Cor. 11:23–26). This is the basic biblical institution:

> Now as they were eating, Jesus took bread, and after blessing it broke it and gave it to the disciples, and said, "Take, eat; this is my body." And he took a cup, and when he had given thanks he gave it to them, saying, "Drink of it, all of you, for this is my blood of the covenant, which is poured out for many for the forgiveness of sins." (Matt. 26:26–28)

Christ's words establish the basic pattern for the Supper, namely, the use of bread to signify his body and wine to signify his blood. As these are respectively broken and poured, testimony is given to Christ's sacrificial death on the cross. Participation takes the form of eating and drinking. Paul further establishes the perpetual observance of the sacrament until the return of Christ: "For as often as you eat this bread and drink the cup, you proclaim the Lord's death until he comes" (1 Cor. 11:26). In reflecting on the biblical institution, we should note the Supper's connection to the Jewish Passover meal and consider its meaning as a sign and as a seal of Christ's new covenant.

The Lord's Supper and Passover

Benjamin Warfield wrote, "Nothing can be more certain than that [Jesus] deliberately chose the Passover meal for the institution of the sacrament of his body and blood."[1] Two passages make clear that Jesus and his disciples were gathered in the Upper Room for the Passover meal (Mark 14:12; Luke 22:7–8). Jesus' clear intention was to connect this new sacrament to its Old Covenant foreshadow.

There are a number of continuities between the two rites. Both are religious feasts in which participation takes the form of eating and drinking. Both focus on an atoning death; indeed, the New Testament teaches that the Paschal lamb typified Jesus Christ in his atoning work (John 1:36; 1 Cor. 5:7; 1 Peter 1:19). Paul says explicitly that the elements of the Lord's Supper "proclaim the Lord's death until he comes" (1 Cor. 11:26). Warfield thus asserts, "The Lord's Supper is the Christian Passover Meal. It takes, and was intended to take, in the Christian Church, the place which the Passover occupied in the Jewish Church. It is the Christian substitute for the Passover."[2]

The Passover was a memorial to Israel's exodus deliverance. The first Passover meal was eaten in Egypt on the night of the plague on the firstborn. Lambs were brought into the Israelite houses to be cared for, indicating an intimacy between the people and the sacrifice (Ex. 12:3). They were to be spotless lambs, which represented fitness to be offered up to the holy God (1 Peter 1:19). The lambs were slaughtered and their blood spread on the sides and tops of the doorframes as a sign, not only for the people but also for God. "When *I* see the blood," said the Lord, "I will pass over you" (Ex. 12:13). That night, while the plague brought terror to the homes of Egypt, the Israelites ate the roasted lamb, with bitter herbs and unleavened bread. "In this manner you shall eat it," they were told, "with your belt fastened, your sandals on your feet, and your staff in your hand. And you shall eat it in haste. It is the LORD'S Passover" (Ex. 12:11).

From the first, the Passover was intended as a perpetual memorial. Prominent in its observance was the removal of yeast not merely from the bread but from the entire household. Unleavened bread is described in Deuteronomy as a symbol of haste and affliction—it could be carried conveniently on a long journey and was the kind of bread one prepared on short notice (Deut. 16:3). The New Testament also understands this as a call to holiness through the removal of sin (1 Cor. 5:6–8).

The Passover feast was to be observed by all the covenant community, but by them only. Slaves or resident aliens could partake only after they had received the covenant mark of circumcision (Ex. 12:43–48). Furthermore, Passover was one of the three feasts for which the people must appear before the Lord in Jerusalem once Israel entered the holy land (Deut. 16:16). By this means, the descendants of Israel would remember the Lord's deliverance in the exodus and the blood that redeemed them from death. Three times in the Book of Exodus, fathers are commanded to tell their children the story of their deliverance by means of the Passover celebration (Ex. 12:26; 13:8; 13:14). While the exodus was a once-for-all, unrepeated act of deliverance, the Passover was a repetitive rite by which successive generations were bound to that salvation. Hughes Old comments, "By participating in the meal, each new generation was added to that people who had been saved from the armies of Pharaoh and the slave-masters of Egypt."[3]

The Lord's Supper as a Sign

Like the Passover, the Lord's Supper was instituted as a sign to the disciples and their future generations. Jesus said, "Do this in remembrance of me" (Luke 22:19; 1 Cor. 11:25). The event signified is the death of Jesus Christ, which our Lord anticipated as imminent. Jesus handed his disciples the bread and said, "This is my body, which is given for you" (Luke 22:19). Then he passed the cup, saying, "This cup that is poured out for you is the new covenant in my blood" (v. 20). Thus the bread and the wine together, as presented with Christ's words, signify Jesus' death for his disciples as an atonement for sin. Charles Hodge observes, "Redemption, therefore, is not by power, or by teaching, or by moral influence, but by expiation. It is this truth which the Lord's Supper exhibits and authenticates."[4] In so doing, our Lord bore testimony to the primacy of his atoning death at the very heart of the Christian religion. According to Louis Berkhof, "The central fact of redemption, prefigured in the sacrifices of the Old Testament, is clearly set forth by means of the significant symbols of the New Testament sacrament. The words of the institution, 'broken for you' and 'shed for many', point to the fact that the death of Christ is a sacrificial one, for the benefit, and even in the place, of His people."[5]

So why did Jesus install a new sacrament, if the Passover already pointed to an atoning death as the source of salvation? The answer is that the central act of redemptive history was unfolding even as the Lord gathered that last time with his disciples. Warfield writes, "He to whom all the Paschal lambs from the beginning had been pointing was about to be offered up. The old things were passing away; behold, all things were to become new."[6] The antitype having come, the type could no longer be fitting to set forth the reality now made new.

A number of changes, Warfield notes, were linked to this great fulfillment and transition. The Jewish state was to be dissolved, along with the ritual law and its sacrifices. In keeping with the finished work of Christ's atoning death, this new sacrament required no altar. Furthermore, in line with the universal character of Christ's salvation, no central location was prescribed. While the symbolism remained essentially the same—propitiation through atoning blood—the symbols were changed to represent the newness of a saving event that would explode the bounds of Israel's prior redemptive experience.[7]

The elements of the Lord's Supper present Christ's death to the senses of his people. But there is more signified in its administration. The eating of the elements by believers signifies their participation in the crucified Christ. Berkhof teaches, "They symbolically appropriate the benefits secured by the sacrificial death of Christ."[8] Additionally, the partaking of the sacrament signifies the effect of Christ's death in giving life and strength to the soul, as food and drink sustain the body. Furthermore, just as the sacrament symbolizes the believers' union with Christ, it also places a visible difference between members of Christ's church and the world, while signifying the believers' communion one to another in him.

The Lord's Supper as a Covenant Seal

The Westminster Confession of Faith refers to this sacrament, as with baptism, as "a holy sign and seal of the covenant of grace" (WCF, XXVII.1). One way to understand the idea of a covenant seal is to realize that the Passover was not merely a religious feast but was also a covenant meal at which God identified with his people, accepted them as his own, and spread before them his provision. We see this happening at numerous times in the Old Testament, but most notably at the ratification of the Mosaic Covenant. The Lord called Moses and Aaron and the seventy elders up onto the mountain, where "they beheld God, and ate and drank" (Ex. 24:11). That the Passover meal served as a covenant renewal is confirmed throughout the Old Testament, through Joshua's celebration of Passover at Gilgal (Josh. 5:10) all the way to Josiah's Passover renewal (2 Kings 23:21–23).

Therefore, when the minister today holds forth the bread and the cup of the Lord's Supper, it is really Christ who sets the meal before his covenant people. Just as the blood marked the houses of those passed over by the angel of death, Jesus marked his disciples as his own, when he held forth the cup and said, "This cup is the new covenant in my blood" (1 Cor. 11:25). By means of his covenant meal, Jesus seals to his disciples the benefits of his atoning death, bringing us into the bonds of his new covenant of salvation. Those who eat and drink of the Lord's Supper, trusting in Christ, receive assurance of his blessing through this seal of his atoning work.

It is the government seal that makes a document official. Thus, the Lord's Supper seals God's people by giving them a reliable attestation of their participation in Christ. Christ thus identifies his own, stretching forth his hand to give them the bread and the cup of his covenant meal. John Murray says, "When we partake of the cup in faith, it is the Lord's own certification to us that all that the new covenant in his blood involves is ours. It is the seal of his grace and faithfulness."[9] Berkhof points out that this sealing assures us that we are the recipients of Christ's atoning work. The Lord's Supper "seals to the participant the great love of Christ . . . it assures the believing participant . . . that he was personally the object of that incomparable love." Furthermore, it confirms to the believer that all the promises of the covenant and all the blessings of salvation "are his in actual possession." Lastly, it is a reciprocal seal whereby believers through participation "profess their faith in Christ as Savior and their allegiance to Him as their King, and they solemnly pledge a life of obedience to His divine commandments."[10]

THEOLOGICAL ISSUES

To surely a majority of believers today, the various theological issues surrounding the Lord's Supper are at best a subject of academic interest and at worst a needless source of division. This marks the difference between our way of thinking and that of our Protestant forebears. To them, the theology of the Lord's Supper was inseparable from the theology of the gospel. If one were to ask such martyrs as Nicholas Ridley and Hugh Latimer, who were burned to death on the formal charge of rejecting the Roman Catholic doctrine of transubstantiation, why they were willing to die for a matter of merely academic interest, they would rightly have replied that what they were dying for was the gospel.

The main theological controversies involving the Lord's Supper have to deal with the question of Christ's presence in the sacrament, the nature of its efficacy as a means of grace, and the question of its necessity. While I will try to treat these as briefly as possible, readers should recognize that these issues have real practical significance in our attitude toward the Lord's Supper and therefore that they cannot safely be neglected.

The Presence of Christ

In what sense is Christ present in the sacrament? There

are three basic views, namely, that Christ is *not present*, that Christ is *physically present*, and that Christ is *spiritually present*.

Christ *not present* in the sacrament. This view is generally attributed to the Swiss Reformer Zwingli, although it fails to do justice to his most mature thought. According to this position the Lord's Supper is a bare sign, a simple commemoration of Christ's atoning death, and an emblem of the believer's trust in him. This position is directed against a mystical or a magical understanding of the Supper, and especially against the corporeal presence of Christ as understood by the Roman Catholic Church. This "memorialist view," as it is sometimes called, holds that the Lord's Supper provides no special grace other than that which faith always receives when the gospel is believed. Undoubtedly, they admit, the sacrament prompts such faith by symbolizing Christ's atoning work, and those who hold the memorialist view reverence the Lord's Supper as a solemn occasion for thanksgiving to the Lord.

Among those who strongly objected to this view was John Calvin, who saw in this an overemphasis on human activity against that of God, as well as on the past work of Christ against his present work through the Holy Spirit.[11] As he pointed out, the memorialist view fails to incorporate all the biblical data, much of which goes beyond mere symbolism. Christ, for instance, did not merely display the elements for the disciples to look at, but he offered them for the disciples to eat. Surely these actions indicate the way in which the sacrament confers blessing and thus demand that we go beyond the memorialist view. Furthermore, the apostle Paul makes plain that partaking this meal involves genuine spiritual reality, so that the recipients participate in the blood and body of Christ (1 Cor. 10:16), and that an unworthy partaker not only offends the Lord but "eats and drinks judgment on himself" (1 Cor. 11:29).

The strength of the Zwinglian or memorialist position is that it protects us from Roman Catholic sacerdotalism and superstition. But it runs into an error of rationalism on the other extreme. It is no surprise, therefore, that this view of the sacrament as a bare memorial often results in the de-emphasis of its importance and in the infrequency of its celebration.

Christ *physically present* in the sacrament. This is the view held by both Roman Catholics and Lutherans, although considerable differences exist between the two. In the Roman view, there is a transformation of the sacramental elements into the corporeal body of Jesus Christ.[12] This is known as *transubstantiation*. Berkhof summarizes, "When the priest utters the formula, '*hoc est corpus meum*', bread and wine change into the body and blood of Christ." The elements continue to look like bread and wine, but in that form the body and blood of Christ are physically present. For this reason, the elevation and adoration of the physical elements of the Supper is justified and encouraged, as indeed it must be. Roman Catholic David Currie explains, "We treat them as we would treat God, because that is what they are."[13] The Roman Catholic Catechism affirms this view, saying, "Under the consecrated species of bread and wine Christ himself, living and glorious, is present in a true, real, and substantial manner: his Body and his Blood, with his soul and his divinity."[14]

Luther rejected this doctrine of transubstantiation, holding instead to a view known as *consubstantiation*. According to him, the elements are not transformed into body and blood, but rather in a mysterious and miraculous way Christ's whole person—body and blood—is present in, under, and along with, the elements of the sacrament. Thus, the physical body of Christ is locally present in the Lord's Supper, although the elements undergo no change. Therefore, while emphasizing the role of faith along with the Zwinglians,

Lutherans also agree with Rome that in the sacrament Christ's body and blood are physically eaten "with the bodily mouth."

Both the Roman and the Lutheran view of the physical presence rely on an absolutely literal interpretation of Christ's words as he handed the bread and the cup to the disciples: "This is my body . . . this is my blood." But contrary to this, it is obvious that the relationship between these elements and Christ's body and blood was representative and sacramental. Jesus was bodily present at the time: it was his hands that held forth the bread; it was before his blood was yet spilled on Calvary that he lifted the cup. Berkhof notes, "It is quite impossible to conceive of the bread which Jesus broke as being the body which was handling it; and it should be noted that Scripture calls it bread even after it is supposed to have been transubstantiated, 1 Cor. 10:17; 11:26–28."[15] The teenage princess Lady Jane Grey made this point to her Catholic interrogator during the reign of Bloody Mary. Reminded that Jesus said, "This is my body," Lady Jane replied: "I grant he saith so; and so he saith, I am the vine, I am the door; but he is never the more for that a door or a vine . . . God forbid that I should say that I eat the very natural body and blood of Christ; for then either I should pluck away my redemption, or else there were two bodies or two Christs, or twelve bodies, when his disciples did eat his body, and it suffered not till the next day."[16]

The Westminster Confession of Faith directs its rejection of Christ's physical presence specifically against the Roman Catholic teaching: "That doctrine which maintains a change of the substance of bread and wine, into the substance of Christ's body and blood (commonly called *transubstantiation*) by consecration of a priest, or by any other way, is repugnant, not to Scripture alone, but even to common sense, and reason; overthroweth the nature of the sacrament, and hath been, and is, the cause of manifold superstitions; yea, of gross idolatries" (WCF, XXIX.6). Calvin adds another important objection: both the Roman and the Lutheran view require Christ's human body to be universally present, so that it partakes in the attributes of divinity. In that case, Christ's true humanity is compromised, so that he is disqualified from his mediatorial work on which our salvation entirely depends. Calvin argues, "Let nothing inappropriate to human nature be ascribed to his body, as happens when it is said either to be infinite or to be put in a number of places at once."[17]

Christ *spiritually present* in the sacrament. Our critique of the memorialist view noticed that the biblical teaching mandates the presence of Christ in some sense (see again 1 Cor. 10:16; 11:29). We do not merely reflect upon Christ's death, but we in some way eat of what is offered. The view that Christ is spiritually present, which is the main Reformed teaching, incorporates this realization along with a rejection of a physical presence. The Westminster Larger Catechism explains, "The body and blood of Christ . . . are spiritually present to the faith of the receiver, no less truly and really than the elements themselves are to their outward senses." Therefore, the communicant "feed[s] upon the body and blood of Christ, not after a corporeal and carnal, but in a spiritual manner; yet truly and really, while by faith they receive and apply to themselves Christ crucified, and all the benefits of his death" (WLC, Q. 170). While the sacramental elements represent Christ's past and completed work on the cross, Christ is present and active through the ministry of the Holy Spirit, through whom he applies the benefits of his atoning death to the hearts of those who receive the sacrament in faith.

The Efficacy of the Sacrament

Inseparable but distinct from the question of Christ's presence is the nature of the sacrament's efficacy (or effectiveness). Here we will first consider *what is the grace conferred* in the Supper, followed by a consideration of *how such grace is communicated.*

The grace conferred. What benefit does the communicant receive through the Lord's Supper? We return to the biblical institution, which indicates that the spiritual benefits we receive in the sacrament are analogous to those benefits received by the body through eating and drinking. In the Lord's Supper, then, the believer is strengthened and fed, receiving sustenance and life. In keeping with the sacrament as a sign, we gain from it a strengthened faith; as a seal of Christ's covenant, we gain increased assurance of salvation and communion with God.

According to Roman Catholics, the Lord's Supper is not only a sacrament, but it is a *sacrifice*, that is, a renewed offering of Christ's death on the cross. Berkhof explains, "The sacrifice of Christ in the Lord's Supper is considered to be a real sacrifice, and is supposed to have propitiatory value."[18] In carefully worded language, the Roman Catholic Catechism denies that a different sacrifice is offered than that of the cross, but rather "it re-presents (makes present) the sacrifice of the cross, because it is its memorial and because it applies its fruit." The Mass is a divine sacrifice wherein Christ "is contained and is offered in an un-bloody manner."[19] As such, the Mass is thought actually to remit sins: just as sins are freshly committed, so the sacrifice of Christ is freshly offered for them in the Mass. This view of the Lord's Supper as a sacrifice must be rejected as denying the vital matter of the sufficiency of Christ's once-for-all atoning death (Rom. 6:10; Heb. 7:27; 9:12, 26; 10:10).

Instead of a sacrifice that propitiates sin, Reformed theology sees the Lord's Supper as conveying grace for the strengthening of faith, for the conveyance of assurance, and for spiritual nourishment and growth (see WCF XIV.1, XXIX.1; WSC 96).

How grace is communicated. Crucial to our understanding of the Lord's Supper is the question of "how it works." The answer is inevitably linked to our view of the Lord's presence in the Supper. In general, we may understand that the memorialist view sees no grace conferred, properly speaking, while the view of Christ's physical presence considers that the physical eating of the elements confers grace. The Reformed doctrine sees the grace conferred by the ministry of the Holy Spirit as Christ is received by faith.

According to Roman Catholics, the benefits of the Lord's Supper are received *ex opere operato*, that is, "by the doing it is done." This is because the grace is contained in the elements themselves, the priest having caused the change of its substance into divine matter. Rome allows that mortal sins may frustrate the sacrament's working of grace, but generally understands that everyone who partakes, regardless of their faith or unbelief, piety or irreligion, automatically receives sacramental grace, including the remission of sins. While Lutherans hold to the necessity of faith, they, too, teach that the sacrament's virtue is inherent in the elements themselves.

In contrast, and in keeping with its teaching of Christ's spiritual presence, Reformed theology understands that through the Lord's Supper the Holy Spirit confers the benefits of Christ's atonement to the believing recipient. The emphasis is not on the corporeal body of Christ but on the bread and the cup signifying his death on our behalf. This is consistent with Christ's own institution, which spoke of his body not merely as such, but as it was given on the cross, and of his blood not as such but as "poured out for you" (Luke 22:20). What the believer feeds upon, then, is not Christ's body as such but the redemptive benefits that he offers through his saving death. The Lord's Supper sets before us Christ crucified, who in the sacrament conveys to our faith all the blessings contained in the giving of his life for those who believe.

The Necessity of the Sacrament

The final theological issue for us briefly to consider is the necessity of the Lord's Supper. Roman Catholics and Lutherans hold that the sacrament is necessary to salvation, in that the grace thus conveyed is not otherwise available. The Reformed view denies this necessity, asserting that the grace received in the sacrament is otherwise available through faith in the Word of the gospel. Berkhof argues this on four considerations. First, given "the free spiritual character of the gospel dispensation . . . God does not bind His grace to the use of certain external forms." Second, he points out that Scripture regards only faith as "an instrumental condition of salvation." Third, the sacraments do not originate faith but presuppose it, and are administered where faith is assumed." Finally, he points out that the Bible shows many people being saved without the sacraments.[20]

The Lord's Supper is therefore not necessary in and of itself as a means of salvation, yet we must acknowledge a necessity resulting from Christ's command. Charles Hodge explains, "No one would be willing to say . . . that it is unnecessary to obey an explicit command of Christ. And as He has commanded his disciples . . . to commemorate his death by the celebration of the Lord's Supper, the strongest moral obligation rests upon his people to obey these commands."[21]

The Confession teaches that the conception of saving faith is not the work of the sacraments, but "is ordinarily wrought by the ministry of the Word." However, it goes on to say that by the Word, "and by the administration of the sacraments, and prayer, [faith] is increased and strengthened" (WCF, XIV.1). Therefore, while the sacraments are not necessary to the initiation of saving faith, the Lord's Supper is necessary, along with the Word and with prayer, for our spiritual nurture and our proper Christian growth.

PASTORAL CONSIDERATIONS

Given the weightiness of the matters we have considered and their implications for a right approach to the Lord's Supper, the need for careful and clear pastoral practice is obvious. Of particular importance here are the sacrament's presentation to the congregation, the right practice of restricted communion, and the worthy partaking of the Lord's Supper by God's people.

Presentation of the Lord's Supper

My first pulpit ministry took place in a church whose weekly services included the celebration of the Lord's Supper. Thus, I concluded each sermon by walking down from the pulpit to the table. Robert Godfrey has written about what a difference it would likely make in much of our preaching "if every sermon had to end in the Lord's Supper. Would it give a healthy new dimension to the way our sermons develop and conclude? Would it force us back to the central things of the gospel?"[22] My experience is that it does. Surely it is a healthy gauge of our preaching to ask whether or not what we have said in the sermon would be of any help in explaining the bread and the wine set forth on the table of the Lord.

It is essential that the physical elements of the Lord's Supper be accompanied by the words of our Lord's institution, normally those given by Paul in 1 Corinthians 11:23–29. This establishes both the authority with which we offer his grace and a biblical explanation of the sacrament's meaning. This should be done simply and without elaboration. Then, the minister should make brief comments pressing upon the people the solemnity of the occasion, perhaps relating the sacrament to the sermon's redemptive message, and briefly instructing the people as to their participation.

Ministers should realize the Lord's Supper's great pastoral value in personally confronting each person present with the reality of his or her own relationship to Jesus Christ. People may endure the sermon with studied indifference; but when the bread and wine are set before them, they must make a decision about what they are going to do. The minister's remarks should bear this in mind, and should directly challenge the people to assess the actual religion they profess. The minister is wise to confront false ways of approaching the Supper, especially those of unbelief and/or works righteousness, but also to encourage the true believer who is faint of heart. Here is the true altar call ministers are to set before the assembled people, where weary Christians are called to revival and unbelievers are confronted with the consequences of their alienation from Christ.

Ministers will find no end of opportunities to connect the Lord's Supper with the redemptive themes of their sermons. This is no surprise, since all of our life in Christ, the whole spectrum of Christian salvation, passes through the cross of our Lord, which is the explicit subject of the Lord's Supper. I would like, however, to suggest a few redemptive themes that are especially connected to the Eucharist and which may serve as examples for the much larger whole of related themes.

I have already mentioned the Passover, and our congregations should be thoroughly familiar with this theme in connection with the Lord's Supper. They should hear of Israel's deliverance from bondage to Pharaoh and our redemption from the Egypt of our sin. They should recall how the lamb's blood turned away God's wrath. They should remember our pilgrim status, and the bitterness of life and the afflictions recalled to us by the unleavened bread. This familiarity should be called forth in song using hymns like this from John of Damascus:

> Come, ye faithful, raise the strain of triumphant gladness
> God hath brought his Israel into joy from sadness;
> Loosed from Pharaoh's bitter yoke Jacob's sons and daughters;
> Led them with unmoistened foot through the Red Sea waters.[23]

It is helpful for ministers to rehearse the events on that night on which our Lord instituted the Supper. We should speak of the dismay with which the disciples heard of the cross, and the words of comfort Jesus gave. Christians should know of the two cups spoken of on that night, the cup of fellowship and gladness offered at the table, and the cup of wrath about which our Lord prayed in the Garden of Gethsemane, a cup he would drink to the bottom. Believers should be directed with hope toward the wedding feast of the Lamb to which we are invited through Jesus' death (Rev. 19:9), the very wine of heaven that in the Supper we now drink by faith.

The Lord's Supper contains within itself a lesson on the history of redemption. It directs us to the past, as our Lord commanded us to "do this in remembrance of me." Christians are people who look back on the death of Christ as the pivotal moment in history. But Christians also look forward, even as Paul tells us, "For as often as you eat this bread and drink the cup, you proclaim the Lord's death until he comes" (1 Cor. 11:26). We are those whose eyes are fixed on the future horizon when our Lord returns in glory and in power. But the sacrament also speaks to the present. Christians gather before the Lord's table like Israel in the desert seeking provision. We are pilgrims on our sojourn to Canaan, and here is the spiritual manna from which we gain strength for the long journey ahead. Here is the drink for the parched lips of our souls, brought forth not by the striking of the rock but by the striking of Christ upon the cross. Like Abraham coming to Melchizedek from the weariness of his battles, we come to Christ to be fed, provisioned, refreshed, and renewed. Horatius Bonar has us therefore sing:

> Here would I feed upon the bread of God,
> Here, drink with thee the royal wine of heaven;
> Here would I lay aside each earthly load,
> Here taste afresh the calm of sin forgiv'n.[24]

Restricted Communion

An important question in administering the Lord's Supper deals with who should partake. Given God's promise of blessing through the sacrament, one might think we should practice open communion, where all may come and partake. But a study of Scripture reveals a clear mandate to restricted communion, to which ministers are bound to adhere and communicants to observe.

John Murray explains the principle of restricted communion, writing, "Not all without distinction are eligible to come to the Lord's Table. . . . When Jesus preached the gospel he made no difference between men. . . . But when he instituted the Lord's Supper he sat down with his disciples. This betokens its distinguishing character; it is for disciples."[25] Murray explains the principles by which the table is to be fenced (or protected):

> The Lord's Supper is chiefly commemoration and communion. It is for those who discern the Lord's body, who can commemorate his death in faith and love. And since the supper is also Communion it is obviously for those who commune with Christ and with one another in the unity of the body which is the church. . . . It is part of the whole counsel of God that those conditions be clearly and insistently set forth, to the end that those who are eligible partake and those who are not refrain.[26]

Who, then, should refrain from the Lord's Supper? First, non-believers must not participate in the sacrament. Paul writes, "Anyone who eats and drinks without discerning the body eats and drinks judgment on himself" (1 Cor. 11:29). This applies as well to Christians who irreverently partake, a particular concern of Paul's in 1 Corinthians, but in general to all who look upon the bread and wine without perceiving their redemptive meaning.

Furthermore, Paul plainly warns against believers who participate in "an unworthy manner," and are thus "guilty of sinning against the body and blood of the Lord" (1 Cor. 11:27 NIV). To guard against this, he says, "Let a person examine himself, then, and so eat of the bread and drink of the cup"

(1 Cor. 11:28). A separate treatment of worthy partaking follows below, but we should note here that Christians are warned to repent of sins that are brought to mind through self-examination. If they are unwilling to repent—and this should be sharply differentiated from weakness in carrying through with repentance—they must refrain from the Supper.

Third, Christians who are under the discipline of the church or who have unreconciled hostility toward another member of the congregation are to refrain from the Supper. The reason for this is that the sacrament is a real participation in the church's spiritual unity. In this respect, frequent communion is a great aid in resolving division in the church and promoting fervent spiritual brotherhood. Calvin observes, "As often as we partake of the symbol of the Lord's body, as a token given and received, we reciprocally bind ourselves to all the duties of love in order that none of us may permit anything to harm our brother, or overlook anything that can help him."[27] Christians ought therefore to prepare for the Supper by seeking reconciliation with others as needed, which is one reason why celebration of the sacrament should be publicized in advance. In the absence of heartfelt fellowship with all others in the congregation, they must then refrain from the Table (see also Jesus' relevant instructions in Matt. 5:23–24).

What about baptized children? Should they participate in the Lord's Supper? A vocal minority today insists that they should. The argument made in support of paedocommunion is threefold: 1) if children of believers are to be baptized, the same logic argues for their admission to the Lord's Supper; 2) in the Old Testament Passover meal, children seem to have eaten along with adults; and 3) Paul's warnings about discerning the body and worthy partaking should be understood as conditioned to the situation of adults and thus having no warrant against children.

It is noteworthy, in response to this challenge, that since the sixteenth century the Reformed churches have been in near universal opposition to paedocommunion, even while acknowledging children's status in the covenant and practicing infant baptism. The reason for this is the difference between a rite of inclusion (baptism) and a rite of communion and fellowship (the Lord's Supper) and the instrumental role of faith involved in the latter. By baptism, a child may be initiated into the church irrespective of his or her faith. Faith, however, is not only necessary to the blessings offered in the Lord's Supper, but without faith the partaking of the sacrament is fruitless at best and blasphemous at worst. The argument for paedocommunion based on infant baptism holds force only if one first accepts baptismal regeneration or some other extreme view of baptismal efficacy.

As for the appeal to the Jewish practice in the Passover meal and other feasts, advocates of paedocommunion fail to note that elements in the *type* do not all pass forward to the *antitype*. For instance, no one who promotes paedocommunion would argue that the Lord's Supper ought to be celebrated only once per year, even though this was the practice for the Passover. Furthermore, this point is vastly overstated. Numerous Old Covenant feasts were restricted to only some covenant members, such as those reserved for priestly families and, especially, the prototypical covenant meal shared only by Moses , Aaron and his sons, and the seventy elders before the Lord (Ex. 24:9–11).

Finally, we should observe that the apostle Paul is quite willing to exclude covenant members from partaking of the Lord's Supper, including those not under discipline. The criterion he employs involves the ability to partake of the sacrament with a proper attitude and understanding (1 Cor. 11:27–31), a criterion that is rightly used to restrict children from partaking.[28] Instead of being brought to the Lord's Table without readiness as biblically described, at an appropriate age baptized children ought to be provided with an opportunity to give a clear and public profession of faith. Only then ought they to participate in Communion.

Worthy Partaking of the Lord's Supper

In 1 Corinthians 11:27–28, Paul warns against partaking of the sacrament in an unworthy manner. His application of this principle extends beyond lack of faith or understanding, for in verse 28, he says "Let a person examine himself, then, and so eat of the bread and drink of the cup." This alerts us to a need for preparation that is broader than doctrinal affirmation only. As Berkhof explains, Paul's teaching indicates that the sacrament is not merely for Christians, but for believers who "earnestly repent of their sins, trust that these have been covered by the atoning blood of Jesus Christ, and are desirous to increase their faith, and to grow in true holiness of life."[29]

A word of caution is in order. Although communicants are warned to approach in a worthy manner, the sacrament does not rely on their spiritual attainment in order "to work"; the blessing is worthily received by faith and not by works. John Calvin thus warns ministers to be sensitive toward believers who are wrongly afflicted by tender consciences. He describes worthy partaking in these words:

> This is the worthiness—the best and only kind we can bring to God—to offer our vileness and our unworthiness to him so that in his mercy we may be taken as worthy; to despair in ourselves so that we may be lifted up by him; to accuse ourselves so that we may be justified by him.[30]

Worthy partaking, then, does not mean making the sacrament "work" in our own spiritual strength, or to present a supposed righteousness of our own, but instead to ensure that ours is a faith that is credible and real. The Westminster Larger Catechism gives us guidance on rightly embracing the sobriety of Communion and on seeking the maximum benefit of this means of grace. Christians should prepare "by examining themselves of their being in Christ, of their sins and wants; of the truth and measure of their knowledge, faith, repentance; love to God and the brethren, charity to all men, forgiving those that have done them wrong; of their desires after Christ, and of their new obedience; and by renewing the exercise of these graces, by serious meditation, and fervent prayer" (WLC, Q. 171). We're also advised to receive the elements "with all holy reverence and attention," and to "affectionately meditate on his death and sufferings . . . in earnest hungering and thirsting after Christ, feeding on him by faith, receiving of his fullness, trusting in his merits, rejoicing in his love, giving thanks for his grace; in renewing of their covenant with God, and love to all the saints" (WLC, Q. 174).

With these things in mind, wise ministers will not only press forth the command to partake worthily, but will urgently remind those present that God's grace is for sinners and not the righteous, for the weak and not the strong, for bad people and not good people. Calvin provides a fitting conclusion to this topic: "It is a sacrament ordained not for the perfect, but for the weak and feeble, to awaken, arouse, stimulate, and exercise the feeling of faith and love, indeed, to correct the defect of both."[31]

CONCLUSION

A thorough consideration of the Lord's Supper reveals the richness of its blessing to the people of God, for which we ought to be moved to the most profound thanksgiving. It also shows how much care must be given to its administration and receipt. The church will be blessed by careful, thoughtful, and expectant preparation, both on the part of the minister in setting forth the sacrament and on the part of those who come in weakness but depart in the strength of the joy of the Lord.

NOTES

1 Benjamin B. Warfield, "The Fundamental Significance of the Lord's Supper" in *Shorter Writings of B. B. Warfield*, 2 vols. (Phillipsburg, N.J.: P&R, 1970), 1:332.
2 Ibid., 1:333.
3 Hughes Oliphant Old, *Worship That Is Reformed According to Scripture* (Atlanta: John Knox, 1984), 106.
4 Charles Hodge, *Systematic Theology*, 3 vols. (Grand Rapids: Eerdmans, 1993), 3:622.
5 Louis Berkhof, *Systematic Theology* (Grand Rapids: Eerdmans, 1939), 650.
6 Warfield, *Shorter Writings*, 1:334.
7 Ibid., 1:333–34.
8 Berkhof, *Systematic Theology*, 650.
9 John Murray, *Collected Writings of John Murray*, 4 vols. (Edinburgh: Banner of Truth, 1977), 2:377.
10 Berkhof, *Systematic Theology*, 651.
11 John Calvin, *Institutes of the Christian Religion*, trans. Ford Lewis Battles (Philadelphia: Westminster, 1960), 4.17.5.
12 Berkhof, *Systematic Theology*, 652.
13 David B. Currie, *Born Fundamentalist, Born Again Catholic* (San Francisco: Ignatius, 1996), 40.
14 *Catechism of the Catholic Church* (New York: Doubleday, 1995), 1413.
15 Berkhof, *Systematic Theology*, 652.
16 Paul F. M. Zahl, *Five Women of the English Reformation* (Grand Rapids: Eerdmans, 2001), 111.

17 Calvin, *Institutes*, 4.17.19.
18 Berkhof, *Systematic Theology*, 655.
19 *Catechism of the Catholic Church*, 1366–7.
20 Berkhof, *Systematic Theology*, 618–19.
21 Hodge, *Systematic Theology*, 3:516.
22 W. Robert Godfrey, "Calvin on the Eucharist," *Modern Reformation* 6, no. 3 (May–June 1997): 48–50 (50).
23 John of Damascus, "Come, Ye Faithful, Raise the Strain," 8th c., Tr. John Mason Neale, 1853.
24 Horatius Bonar, "Here, O My Lord, I See Thee Face to Face," 1855.
25 Murray, *Collected Writings*, 3:275.
26 Ibid., 2:381.
27 Calvin, *Institutes*, 4.17.44.
28 I was assisted here by an *In thesi* Statement on Paedocommunion prepared by the Mississippi Valley Presbytery of the Presbyterian Church in America, provided to me by Dr. J. Ligon Duncan III.
29 Berkhof, *Systematic Theology*, 656.
30 Calvin, *Institutes*, 4.17.42.
31 Ibid.